BREAKTHROUGH TO MATH

EXPONENTS, ROOTS, AND POLYNOMIALS

LEVEL 3

Materials were developed by Rowan College
(formerly Glassboro State College) in cooperation
with New Jersey State Department of Education,
Division of School Programs, Bureau of Adult
Continuing Education.

Materials do not necessarily reflect the policy of the
New Jersey State Department of Education and no
official endorsement should be inferred.

BOOK
1 2 3
4 5

Edited by Ann K.U. Tussing

Curriculum developers:
Barbara Banks, Loretta Pullano

New Readers Press

Table of contents

Breakthrough to Math Level 3
Exponents, Roots, and Polynomials
ISBN 978-0-88336-833-6

Copyright © 1983, 1978 Rowan College (formerly Glassboro State College)

Published and distributed by:
New Readers Press
A Publishing Division of ProLiteracy
1320 Jamesville Avenue, Syracuse, New York 13210
www.newreaderspress.com

Printed in the United States of America
20   19   18   17   16   15   14   13   12

All proceeds from the sale of New Readers Press materials
support literacy programs in the United States and worldwide.

Designers: Caris Lester, Marsha Shur, and Helen Lannis
Typesetter: Jeanann Georgianna

Pre-test

1. List the factors of 100.

_____

2. Circle the correct answer.

   $(-5)^3$ stands for

   a. $(-5)(3)$

   b. $(-5)(-5)(-5)$

   c. $(-5)+(3)$

3. Find the value of 5^3.

   _____

4. $\sqrt{49}$ = _____

5. List the terms in this expression:
   $2xy + 5xy - 3ab^2 + yz$

   _____

6. List any like terms in this expression:
   $x^2 + 3mn + 2mn + m^2n$

   _____

7. Combine: $5t + 7t$ = _____

8. Combine: $11pt - (-8pt)$ = _____

9. $\left(-\frac{1}{2}a\right)(-4a^2b)$ = _____

10. $\dfrac{15x^4}{3x^2}$ = _____

11. $(x^2 + 2xy - 5y^2) + (4x^2 - 3xy + 7y^2)$ =

    _____

12. $(4x^2 - 5xy - y^2) - (3x^2 + 5xy + y^2)$ =

    _____

13. $-4(4b^2 - 5bc + 3c^2)$ =

    _____

14. $(x + 3)(x + 2)$ =

    _____

15. $\dfrac{15b^3 - 21b^2 - 9b}{3b}$ = _____

16. Factor: $(abc + abd + abf)$

    _____

17. Multiply: $(a + 8)(a - 8)$ =

    _____

18. Factor: $(x^2 - 25)$

    _____

Answers for pre-test

1. 1, 2, 4, 5, 10, 20, 25, 50, 100
2. b
3. 125
4. 7
5. $2xy$, $5xy$, $3ab^2$, yz
6. $3mn$, $2mn$
7. $12t$
8. $19pt$
9. $2a^3b$

10. $5x^2$
11. $5x^2 - xy + 2y^2$
12. $x^2 - 10xy - 2y^2$
13. $-16b^2 + 20bc - 12c^2$
14. $x^2 + 5x + 6$
15. $5b^2 - 7b - 3$
16. $ab(c + d + f)$
17. $a^2 - 64$
18. $(x + 5)(x - 5)$

If you missed this question:	Study these pages:
1	➤ 6-8
2 or 3	➤ 9-12
4	➤ 13-15
5 or 6	➤ 16-18
7 or 8	➤ 19-22
9	➤ 23-27
10	➤ 28-32
11	➤ 33-35
12	➤ 36-38
13	➤ 39-42
14	➤ 43-46
15	➤ 47-49
16	➤ 50-53
17	➤ 54-56
18	➤ 57-60

1. Factors

When you multiply two or more numbers together, the answer is called the product.
The numbers that are multiplied together are called *factors*.

(12)(2) = 24
The product is 24.
12 and 2 are factors of 24.
Other numbers can be multiplied together to equal 24.

(3)(8) = 24
(4)(6) = 24
(24)(1) = 24

So, 1, 2, 3, 4, 6, 8, 12, and 24 are all factors of 24.
All of those numbers divide evenly into 24.

When you "factor a number", you are finding the numbers which, when multiplied together, equal the given number.
When working with whole numbers, we will find only the factors that are whole numbers.
So, the factors of a given whole number are the numbers that divide evenly into that given number.

Practice with factors

Example 1.   Find the factors of 100.
Think of the numbers that divide evenly into 100.
(1)(100) = 100
(2)(50) = 100
(4)(25) = 100
(5)(20) = 100
(10)(10) = 100
So, the factors of 100 are 1, 2, 4, 5, 10, 20, 25, 50, and 100.

Example 2. Factor: -16.

The product is a negative number.

To get a negative product, multiply a positive number by a negative number.

$$(-4)(4) = -16$$
$$(-2)(8) = -16$$
$$(2)(-8) = -16$$
$$(16)(-1) = -16$$
$$(-16)(1) = -16$$

Each of the factors could be positive or negative.

This sign before a number stands for "positive or negative": $\pm$.

So, the factors of -16 are ±1, ±2, ±4, ±8, and ±16.

Exercise 1

Factor these numbers.

For negative products, use the "positive or negative sign" in your answers.

1. $36 =$ ( )( )
   ( )( )
   ( )( )
   ( )( )
   ( )( )

2. $48 =$ ( )( )
   ( )( )
   ( )( )
   ( )( )
   ( )( )

3. $-20 =$ ( )( )
   ( )( )
   ( )( )

4. $60 =$ ( )( )
   ( )( )
   ( )( )
   ( )( )
   ( )( )
   ( )( )

5. $-25 =$ ( )( )
   ( )( )

6. $21 =$ ( )( )
   ( )( )

Answers for exercise 1

1. $36 = (1)(36)$
   $(2)(18)$
   $(3)(12)$
   $(4)(9)$
   $(6)(6)$

2. $48 = (1)(48)$
   $(2)(24)$
   $(3)(16)$
   $(4)(12)$
   $(6)(8)$

3. $-20 = (\pm 1)(\pm 20)$
   $(\pm 2)(\pm 10)$
   $(\pm 4)(\pm 5)$

4. $60 = (1)(60)$
   $(2)(30)$
   $(3)(20)$
   $(4)(15)$
   $(5)(12)$
   $(6)(10)$

5. $-25 = (\pm 1)(\pm 25)$
   $(\pm 5)(\pm 5)$

6. $21 = (1)(21)$
   $(3)(7)$

2. Exponents

In algebra, when you multiply a number times itself, you use exponents to show that multiplication.

An exponent is a number written to the right and slightly above the number you are multiplying.

The number you are multiplying is called the base number.

The exponent tells how many times the base number is a factor.

5^2 —exponent
5 —base number

The base number is 5.

The exponent is 2.

The exponent 2 tells you that 5 is a factor 2 times.

$5^2 = (5)(5) = 25$

When the exponent is 2, we say the base number is being squared.

Read 5^2 as "five squared."

If the exponent is 3, we say the base number is being cubed.

Read 5^3 as "five cubed."

The exponent 3 tells you that 5 is a factor 3 times.

$5^3 = (5)(5)(5) = 125$

A number can be multiplied any number of times.

5^6 means the base number 5 is a factor 6 times.

Read 5^6 as "five to the power of six."

$5^6 = (5)(5)(5)(5)(5)(5) = 15,625$

Fractions or decimals can have exponents.

$.03^3$ means the base number .03 is a factor 3 times.

Read $.03^3$ as "three hundredths cubed."

$.03^3 = (.03)(.03)(.03) = .000027$

Practice with exponents

Example 1. $7^4 =$

Step 1.   The base number is 7 and the exponent is 4.
Write 7 as a factor 4 times.
$(7)(7)(7)(7)$

Step 2.   Multiply.
$(7)(7)(7)(7) = 2,401$
So, $7^4 = 2,401$

Example 2. $-9^3 =$

Step 1.   The base number is -9 and the exponent is 3.
Write -9 as a factor 3 times.
$(-9)(-9)(-9)$

Step 2.   Multiply.
$(-9)(-9)(-9) = -729$
So, $-9^3 = -729$

If the base number is negative, and the exponent is an odd number, the product will be negative.

Example 3. $-2^4 =$

Step 1.   The base number is -2 and the exponent is 4.
Write -2 as a factor 4 times.
$(-2)(-2)(-2)(-2)$

Step 2.   Multiply.
$(-2)(-2)(-2)(-2) = 16$
So, $-2^4 = 16$

If the base number is negative and the exponent is an even number, the product will be positive.

Example 4. $\left(\frac{1}{2}\right)^4 =$

Step 1.   The base number is $\frac{1}{2}$, and the exponent is 4.
Write $\frac{1}{2}$ as a factor 4 times.
$\left(\frac{1}{2}\right) \left(\frac{1}{2}\right) \left(\frac{1}{2}\right) \left(\frac{1}{2}\right)$

Step 2.   Multiply.
$\left(\frac{1}{2}\right) \left(\frac{1}{2}\right) \left(\frac{1}{2}\right) \left(\frac{1}{2}\right) = \frac{1}{16}$
So, $\left(\frac{1}{2}\right)^4 = \frac{1}{16}$

Exercise 2

Find the value of these numbers.

1. $8^3 =$

2. $5^5 =$

3. $(-2)^6 =$

4. $4^4 =$

5. $(-7)^3 =$

6. $(-3)^5 =$

7. $(-4)^2 =$

8. $11^3 =$

Answers for exercise 2

1. $8^3 = (8)(8)(8) = 512$

2. $5^5 = (5)(5)(5)(5)(5) = 3,125$

3. $(-2)^6 = (-2)(-2)(-2)(-2)(-2)(-2) = 64$

4. $4^4 = (4)(4)(4)(4) = 256$

5. $(-7)^3 = (-7)(-7)(-7) = -343$

6. $(-3)^5 = (-3)(-3)(-3)(-3)(-3) = -243$

7. $(-4)^2 = (-4)(-4) = 16$

8. $11^3 = (11)(11)(11) = 1,331$

3. Square roots

When you find the square root of a given number, you are finding what number times itself equals that given number.
For example, the square root of 25 is 5 because 5 times itself equals 25.

$5^2 = (5)(5) = 25$

The symbol for square root is $\sqrt{}$.

$\sqrt{25} = 5$ Read that as "the square root of 25 is 5."

Practice finding square roots

Example 1. $\sqrt{81} =$
What number times itself equals 81?
$9^2 = (9)(9) = 81$.
So, $\sqrt{81} = 9$

Example 2. $\sqrt{\frac{9}{16}} =$
Find the square root of the numerator (top number).
Then find the square root of the denominator (bottom number).

$\frac{\sqrt{9}}{\sqrt{16}} = \frac{3}{4}$

So, $\sqrt{\frac{9}{16}} = \frac{3}{4}$

Example 3.   Square roots do not always come out evenly.
You might have a chart (see page 14) or a calculator to help you find square roots.
Or you might have to estimate the square root.

$\sqrt{90} =$
Try a few whole numbers to see what numbers, when multiplied together, come close to the product, 90.
$(9)(9) = 81$
$(10)(10) = 100$
The square root of 90 is between 9 and 10.
Try some numbers between 9 and 10.

$9.2^2 = 84.64$
$9.3^2 = 86.49$
$9.4^2 = 88.36$
$9.5^2 = 90.25$

So, $\sqrt{90} =$ about 9.5

The square roots in this chart have been rounded off to the nearest thousandth.

$\sqrt{1} = 1.000$	$\sqrt{26} = 5.099$	$\sqrt{51} = 7.141$	$\sqrt{76} = 8.718$
$\sqrt{2} = 1.414$	$\sqrt{27} = 5.196$	$\sqrt{52} = 7.211$	$\sqrt{77} = 8.775$
$\sqrt{3} = 1.732$	$\sqrt{28} = 5.292$	$\sqrt{53} = 7.280$	$\sqrt{78} = 8.832$
$\sqrt{4} = 2.000$	$\sqrt{29} = 5.385$	$\sqrt{54} = 7.348$	$\sqrt{79} = 8.888$
$\sqrt{5} = 2.236$	$\sqrt{30} = 5.477$	$\sqrt{55} = 7.416$	$\sqrt{80} = 8.944$
$\sqrt{6} = 2.449$	$\sqrt{31} = 5.568$	$\sqrt{56} = 7.483$	$\sqrt{81} = 9.000$
$\sqrt{7} = 2.646$	$\sqrt{32} = 5.657$	$\sqrt{57} = 7.550$	$\sqrt{82} = 9.055$
$\sqrt{8} = 2.828$	$\sqrt{33} = 5.745$	$\sqrt{58} = 7.616$	$\sqrt{83} = 9.110$
$\sqrt{9} = 3.000$	$\sqrt{34} = 5.831$	$\sqrt{59} = 7.681$	$\sqrt{84} = 9.165$
$\sqrt{10} = 3.162$	$\sqrt{35} = 5.916$	$\sqrt{60} = 7.746$	$\sqrt{85} = 9.220$
$\sqrt{11} = 3.317$	$\sqrt{36} = 6.000$	$\sqrt{61} = 7.810$	$\sqrt{86} = 9.274$
$\sqrt{12} = 3.464$	$\sqrt{37} = 6.083$	$\sqrt{62} = 7.874$	$\sqrt{87} = 9.327$
$\sqrt{13} = 3.606$	$\sqrt{38} = 6.164$	$\sqrt{63} = 7.937$	$\sqrt{88} = 9.381$
$\sqrt{14} = 3.742$	$\sqrt{39} = 6.245$	$\sqrt{64} = 8.000$	$\sqrt{89} = 9.434$
$\sqrt{15} = 3.873$	$\sqrt{40} = 6.325$	$\sqrt{65} = 8.062$	$\sqrt{90} = 9.487$
$\sqrt{16} = 4.000$	$\sqrt{41} = 6.403$	$\sqrt{66} = 8.124$	$\sqrt{91} = 9.539$
$\sqrt{17} = 4.123$	$\sqrt{42} = 6.481$	$\sqrt{67} = 8.185$	$\sqrt{92} = 9.592$
$\sqrt{18} = 4.243$	$\sqrt{43} = 6.557$	$\sqrt{68} = 8.246$	$\sqrt{93} = 9.644$
$\sqrt{19} = 4.359$	$\sqrt{44} = 6.633$	$\sqrt{69} = 8.307$	$\sqrt{94} = 9.695$
$\sqrt{20} = 4.472$	$\sqrt{45} = 6.708$	$\sqrt{70} = 8.367$	$\sqrt{95} = 9.747$
$\sqrt{21} = 4.583$	$\sqrt{46} = 6.782$	$\sqrt{71} = 8.426$	$\sqrt{96} = 9.798$
$\sqrt{22} = 4.690$	$\sqrt{47} = 6.856$	$\sqrt{72} = 8.485$	$\sqrt{97} = 9.849$
$\sqrt{23} = 4.796$	$\sqrt{48} = 6.928$	$\sqrt{73} = 8.544$	$\sqrt{98} = 9.899$
$\sqrt{24} = 4.899$	$\sqrt{49} = 7.000$	$\sqrt{74} = 8.602$	$\sqrt{99} = 9.950$
$\sqrt{25} = 5.000$	$\sqrt{50} = 7.071$	$\sqrt{75} = 8.660$	$\sqrt{100} = 10.000$

Exercise 3

Use the chart to find the square roots
of these numbers.

1. $\sqrt{12} =$

2. $\sqrt{50} =$

3. $\sqrt{80} =$

4. $\sqrt{\frac{1}{4}} =$

5. $\sqrt{20} =$

6. $\sqrt{69} =$

7. $\sqrt{27} =$

8. $\sqrt{39} =$

9. $\sqrt{99} =$

10. $\sqrt{22} =$

Estimate these square roots to the nearest tenth.

11. $\sqrt{250} =$

12. $\sqrt{220} =$

13. $\sqrt{300} =$

14. $\sqrt{280} =$

Answers for exercise 3

1. $\sqrt{12} = 3.464$

2. $\sqrt{50} = 7.071$

3. $\sqrt{80} = 8.944$

4. $\sqrt{\frac{1}{4}} = \frac{1}{2}$

5. $\sqrt{20} = 4.472$

6. $\sqrt{69} = 8.307$

7. $\sqrt{27} = 5.196$

8. $\sqrt{39} = 6.245$

9. $\sqrt{99} = 9.950$

10. $\sqrt{22} = 4.690$

11. $\sqrt{250} = 15.8$

12. $\sqrt{220} = 14.8$

13. $\sqrt{300} = 17.3$

14. $\sqrt{280} = 16.7$

4. Terms

An equation is a number sentence.
It tells about equal things.
An expression is part of an equation.
This is an equation: $3x + 3 = 24$.
This is an expression: $3x + 3$.

An expression is made up of smaller parts called *terms*.
In the equation above, $3x$, 3, and 24 are all terms.
A term can be made up of numbers, variables, or numbers and variables.
A term can have exponents in it, too: $3x^2$, $2ab^2c$.

An expression that is made up of only one term is called a *monomial*.
An expression that is made up of more than one term is called a *polynomial*.
This is a monomial or term: $3xb$.
This is a polynomial with three terms: $(x^2 + 5x + 6)$.

Terms are *held together* by multiplying or dividing.
These terms are held together by multiplying: $2a$, a^2b, $7xy$, $2(x + y)$.
These terms are held together by dividing: $\frac{b}{a}$, $\frac{2a}{xy}$, $\frac{x}{y}$, $\frac{x^3}{2}$

Terms are usually *separated* by adding or subtracting.
This polynomial or expression has four terms: $2a^2b + xy - 8 - \frac{b}{c}$
The plus and minus signs separate the terms.
But $2(x + y)$ is one term because multiplication holds it together.
The parentheses show multiplication.

Terms with all the same variables and exponents are called *like terms*.
These are sets of like terms: $7a$, $2a$

$$ab^2,\ 3ab^2,\ -2ab^2$$
$$x^2y^3z^4,\ 4x^2y^3z^4$$
$$\frac{y}{x},\ 2\frac{y}{x}$$

Terms with different variables and exponents are *unlike terms*.
These are unlike terms: x^2y, and xy.
The two terms have the same variables, but the exponents are different.

Practice with terms

How many terms are there in each expression?
What are the like terms?

Example 1. $2d^2c + 8 - 5d^2c + 8x + 2$
In this expression, there are five terms.
There are two pairs of like terms: $2d^2c$, $5d^2c$
8, 2.

Example 2. $2x^2 + 3x - 8 + 3x^2 - 4x^2$
There are five terms.
There are three like terms: $2x^2$, $3x^2$, $4x^2$.

Example 3. $3xy + 2ab^2 - xy + ab^2$
There are four terms.
There are two pairs of like terms: $3xy$, xy
$2ab^2$, ab^2.

Exercise 4

For each expression below, tell how many terms there are and identify any like terms.

Number of terms   *Like terms*

1. $6a - 9x + 3x - 3a$

2. $4 - 10x + 2$

3. $2x^2 + 3b^2 - 4 + x^2 + b^2$

4. $-11d^2 + 8 - 11d + 11d^3$

5. $7y - 8a + 4a - \dfrac{a}{y} + \dfrac{y}{a}$

6. $xt^2 - x^2t^2 + 30x$

7. $\dfrac{x^2}{b} - \dfrac{x}{b} + 2x^2 - 2\dfrac{x^2}{b}$

Answers for exercise 4

	Number of terms	Like terms
1. $6a - 9x + 3x - 3a$	four	$6a, 3a$ $9x, 3x$
2. $4 - 10x + 2$	three	$4, 2$
3. $2x^2 + 3b^2 - 4 + x^2 + b^2$	five	$2x^2, x^2$ $3b^2, b^2$
4. $-11d^2 + 8 - 11d + 11d^3$	four	none
5. $7y - 8a + 4a - \frac{a}{y} + \frac{y}{a}$	five	$8a, 4a$
6. $xt^2 - x^2t^2 + 30x$	three	none
7. $\frac{x^2}{b} - \frac{x}{b} + 2x^2 - 2\frac{x^2}{b}$	four	$\frac{x^2}{b}, 2\frac{x^2}{b}$

5. Adding and subtracting monomials

Monomials are algebraic expressions of one term only.
You can add and subtract monomials if they are like terms.

You can add $3ab^2$ and $5ab^2$ because they are like terms.
But you can't add $3ab + 5ab^2$ because the terms are unlike.

Adding monomials with like terms

To add monomials, first combine the numbers in front of the terms.
Follow the rules for adding signed numbers.
If the signs are the same, keep that sign and add the numbers.
If the signs are different, subtract the smaller number from the larger number
and use the sign of the larger in the answer.
After adding the numbers, simply write the variable in the answer exactly as it
appears in the problem.

$7x^2 + 3x^2 =$

Step 1.　　Add the numbers:

$$7x^2 + 3x^2 = 10$$

Step 2.　　Write the variable next to the answer:

$$7x^2 + 3x^2 = 10x^2$$

So, $7x^2 + 3x^2 = 10x^2$

Subtracting monomials with like terms

To subtract monomials, first combine the numbers in front of the terms.
Follow the rules for subtracting signed numbers.
Change the sign of the second number and add.
Then write the variable in the answer exactly as it appears in the problem.

$12ab^2 - (-3ab^2) =$

Step 1.　　Subtract the numbers.

To subtract, change the sign of the second number and add:
$$12ab^2 + (+3ab^2) = 15$$

Step 2.　　Write the variable next to the answer.

$$12ab^2 + 3ab^2 = 15ab^2$$

So, $12ab^2 - (-3ab^2) = 15ab^2$

Practice adding and subtracting monomials

Problems can be vertical (up and down) or horizontal (across).

Example 1.
$$\begin{array}{r} -3abc^2 \\ +\quad abc^2 \\ \hline \end{array}$$

Combine the numbers in front of the variables.
Then write the variables after the answer.
Remember, when there is no number in front of a variable, a 1 is understood.

$$\begin{array}{r} -3abc^2 \\ +\quad 1abc^2 \\ \hline -2abc^2 \end{array}$$

So,
$$\begin{array}{r} -3abc^2 \\ +\quad abc^2 \\ \hline -2abc^2 \end{array}$$

Example 2. $-5prt - (-5prt) =$
To subtract, change the sign of the term after the subtraction sign, and add.

$-5prt + (+5prt) = 0prt = 0$

(0 times a number or variable is always 0.)
So, $-5prt - (-5prt) = 0$

Example 3. $(8bc) - (10bc) + (3bc) - (-bc) =$

Step 1.   Look for the subtraction signs.
Change the signs of the terms after the subtraction signs so that you can add.

$(8bc) + (-10bc) + (3bc) + (+bc) = 2bc$

Step 2.   Add the positive terms.
$(8bc) + (3bc) + (1bc) = 12bc$

Step 3.   There is only one negative term: $-10bc$.
Add the positive and negative sums.

$(12bc) + (-10bc) = 2bc$

So, $(8bc) + (-10bc) + (3bc) + (+bc) = 2bc$

Example 4. $5x^3y + 2xy - 3x^3y + 2 =$

Sometimes, there are like and unlike terms in a problem.

Step 1.   Combine the like terms.

$5x^3y + 2xy - 3x^3y + 2 = 2x^3y$

Step 2.   Write the unlike terms in the answer exactly as they appear in the problem.
Be sure to keep the right signs with them.

$5x^3y + 2xy - 3x^3y + 2 = 2x^3y + 2xy + 2$

So, $5x^3y + 2xy - 3x^3y + 2 = 2x^3y + 2xy + 2$

Exercise 5

Combine these monomials.

1. $3x^2 + x^2 + x^2 =$

2. $ab^2 + ab^4 - 3ab^2 + ab^4 =$

3. $m + m + n^2 =$

4. $7y^5 - 6x + 2y^5 - 2 =$

5. $-8x + 9z^2 + 2 + z^2 =$

6. $7a^2y - 4a^2y - 3a^2y + a^2y =$

7. $3\dfrac{a}{b} + 2\dfrac{a}{b} - \dfrac{a}{b} + \dfrac{a^2}{b} =$

8. $\begin{array}{r} 5rs \\ -\ -8rs \\ \hline \end{array}$

9. $\begin{array}{r} -7a^2b^2 \\ -\ \ \ 4a^2b^2 \\ \hline \end{array}$

10. $\begin{array}{r} -8cd^2 \\ -\ -8cd^2 \\ \hline \end{array}$

Answers for exercise 5

1. $3x^2 + x^2 + x^2 = 5x^2$

2. $ab^2 + ab^4 - 3ab^2 + ab^4 = -2ab^2 + 2ab^4$

3. $m + m + n^2 = 2m + n^2$

4. $7y^5 - 6x + 2y^5 - 2 = 9y^5 - 6x - 2$

5. $-8x + 9z^2 + 2 + z^2 = -8x + 10z^2 + 2$

6. $7a^2y - 4a^2y - 3a^2y + a^2y = a^2y$

7. $3\dfrac{a}{b} + 2\dfrac{a}{b} - \dfrac{a}{b} + \dfrac{a^2}{b} = 4\dfrac{a}{b} + \dfrac{a^2}{b}$

8.
$$\begin{array}{r} 5rs \\ -\ -8rs \\ \hline 13rs \end{array}$$

9.
$$\begin{array}{r} -7a^2b^2 \\ -\ \ \ 4a^2b^2 \\ \hline -11a^2b^2 \end{array}$$

10.
$$\begin{array}{r} -8cd^2 \\ -\ -8cd^2 \\ \hline 0 \end{array}$$

6. Multiplying monomials

When you multiply monomials, you can multiply like or unlike terms.
Multiply the numbers in front of the variables first.
If there is no number in front of a variable, a 1 is understood.
That is, x is the same as $1x$.
Then multiply the variables together.
Multiply the variables by adding the exponents.
If a variable doesn't have an exponent, then an exponent of 1 is understood.
x is the same as x^1.

$(4x)(x^2) =$

Step 1.   Multiply the numbers in front of the variables.
           There is no number in front of x^2, so a 1 is understood.

$$(4x)(1x^2) = 4$$

Step 2.   Multiply the variables by adding the exponents.
           $4x$ has no exponent, so an exponent of 1 is understood: $1 + 2 = 3$.

$$4x^1(x^2) = 4x^3$$
$$\text{So, } (4x)(x^2) = 4x^3$$

Here's why you add exponents.
An exponent tells how many times the base is a factor.

You could multiply the whole thing out:

$$\begin{array}{cc} (x) & (x)(x) \\ x^1 & x^2 \end{array}$$

Then you could count the x's to find out how many times x is a factor—3 times.
When x is a factor 3 times, you write x^3.
It is quicker to add the exponents.

Sometimes, there is more than one variable in a monomial.

$2xb^2(3x^2b^2) =$

Step 1.   Multiply the numbers.

$$(2xb^2)(3x^2b^2) = 6$$

Step 2.   Multiply the variables.
Multiply the letters one at a time, by adding the exponents of like variables.
Multiply the x's by adding the variables: $1 + 2 = 3$.

$$(2x^1b^2)(3x^2b^2) = 6x^3$$

Multiply the b's by adding the variables: $2 + 2 = 4$

$$(2xb^2)(3x^2b^2) = 6x^3b^4$$

So, $(2xb^2)(3x^2b^2) = 6x^3b^4$

If a variable appears in only one of the terms, write that variable and its exponent in the answer exactly as it appears in the term.

$(-4m^2n^3)(-2n^2) =$

Step 1.   Multiply the numbers.

$$(-4m^2n^3)(-2n^2) = 8$$

Step 2.   Multiply the variables.
There are no m's in the second term.
So, write the m^2 from the first term in the answer.
$(-4m^2n^3)(-2n^2) = 8m^2$
Multiply the n's by adding exponents: $3 + 2 = 5$.

$$(-4m^2n^3)(-2n^2) = 8m^2n^5$$

So, $(-4m^2n^3)(-2n^2) = 8m^2n^5$

Practice multiplying monomials

Example 1. $(5ac)(-2ac) =$

Step 1.   Multiply the numbers.

$$(5ac)(-2ac) = -10$$

Step 2.   Multiply the variables.
Remember, if there is no exponent, an exponent of 1
is understood.
Multiply the a's by adding exponents: $1 + 1 = 2$.

$$(5a^1c)(-2a^1c) = -10a^2$$

Multiply the c's by adding exponents: $1 + 1 = 2$.

$$(5a^1c^1)(-2a^1c^1) = -10a^2c^2$$
$$\text{So, } (5ac)(-2ac) = -10a^2c^2$$

Example 2. $(-7p^4r^2t^2)(.04p^2r^3t^3) =$

Step 1.   Multiply the numbers.

$$(-7p^4r^2t^2)(.04p^2r^3t^3) = -.28$$

Step 2.   Multiply the variables by adding exponents.
Multiply the p's.

$$(-7p^4r^2t^2)(.04p^2r^3t^3) = -.28p^6$$

Multiply the r's.

$$(-7p^4r^2t^2)(.04p^2r^3t^3) = -.28p^6r^5$$

Multiply the t's.

$$(-7p^4r^2t^2)(.04p^2r^3t^3) = -.28p^6r^5t^5$$
$$\text{So, } (-7p^4r^2t^2)(.04p^2r^3t^3) = -.28p^6r^5t^5$$

Example 3. $(-5x^2y^2)(\frac{1}{5}y) =$

Step 1. Multiply the numbers.

$$(-5x^2y^2)(\frac{1}{5}y) = -1$$

Step 2. Multiply the variables.
There is no x in the second term, so simply write x^2 in the answer.

$$(-5x^2y^2)(\frac{1}{5}y) = -1x^2$$

Multiply the y's by adding exponents.

$$(-5x^2y^2)(\frac{1}{5}y^1) = -1x^2y^3 = -x^2y^3$$

So, $(-5x^2y^2)(\frac{1}{5}y) = -x^2y^3$

Exercise 6

Multiply these numbers.

1. $(-7mn)(-8mn) =$

2. $(5)(a^2b^2) =$

3. $(-\frac{1}{2}ab)(8b) =$

4. $(4p^2)(7rt) =$

5. $(-9a^3)(-3a^3) =$

6. $(-3dx^4)(3d) =$

7. $(-6x^3)(4x^4) =$

8. $(.2xy)(.2x) =$

9. $(ab)(-4a^2) =$

10. $(7bt^4n^5)(-3b^3tn^2) =$

Answers for exercise 6

1. $(-7mn)(-8mn) = 56m^2n^2$

2. $(5)(a^2b^2) = 5a^2b^2$

3. $(-\frac{1}{2}ab)(8b) = -4ab^2$

4. $(4p^2)(7rt) = 28p^2rt$

5. $(-9a^3)(-3a^3) = 27a^6$

6. $(-3dx^4)(3d) = -9d^2x^4$

7. $(-6x^3)(4x^4) = -24x^7$

8. $(.2xy)(.2x) = .04x^2y$

9. $(ab)(-4a^2) = -4a^3b$

10. $(7bt^4n^5)(-3b^3tn^2) = -21b^4t^5n^7$

7. Dividing monomials

To divide monomials, first divide the numbers in front of the variables.
Remember, if there is no number, then a 1 is understood.
Then divide the variables.
Divide variables by *subtracting* exponents.
Remember, if there is no exponent, then an exponent of 1 is understood.

$$\frac{-21x^4}{3x^2} =$$

Step 1.   Divide the numbers:

$$\frac{-21x^4}{3x^2} = -7$$

Step 2.   Divide the variables by subtracting the exponents: $4 - 2 = 2$.

$$\frac{-21x^4}{3x^2} = -7x^2$$

$$\text{So, } \frac{-21x^4}{3x^2} = -7x^2$$

Here's why you subtract exponents.
The exponent tells you how many times the base is a factor.
Write out the x's as factors.
Keep the problem set up as a division problem.

$$\frac{\overset{1}{(\cancel{x})}\overset{1}{(\cancel{x})}(x)(x)}{\underset{1}{(\cancel{x})}\underset{1}{(\cancel{x})}}$$

The x's on the bottom cancel out two x's on top.
Two x's are left; that is, x is a factor 2 times.
Write that with an exponent: x^2.
That is the same answer you got when you subtracted exponents.

Suppose the variable and exponent are the same in the two monomials you are dividing.

When you divide a number by itself, you get 1.

$$\frac{x^2}{x^2} = 1$$

Write the problem with x as a factor twice in the numerator and twice in the denominator.

$$\frac{\overset{1}{(\cancel{x})}\overset{1}{(\cancel{x})}}{\underset{1}{(\cancel{x})}\underset{1}{(\cancel{x})}} = 1$$

The x's all cancel out, leaving 1.

If you had subtracted the exponents, you would have gotten 0.
So, x^0 is the same as 1.

Sometimes, the variable appears in only one of the terms being divided.
Then write the variable and exponent in the answer exactly as it appears in the problem.
If the extra variable is on the bottom, keep it on the bottom.

$$\frac{x^2 y}{xyz} =$$

Step 1.   Divide the x's.

$$\frac{x^2 y}{xyz} = \frac{x}{}$$

Step 2.   Divide the y's.
They cancel out.

$$\frac{x^2 \cancel{y}}{x\cancel{y}z} = \frac{x}{}$$

Step 3. z is on the bottom only, so write it in the answer.

$$\frac{x^2 y}{xyz} = \frac{x}{z}$$

So, $\dfrac{x^2 y}{xyz} = \dfrac{x}{z}$

Practice dividing monomials

Example 1. $\dfrac{-6x^3y^2z}{-3xz} =$

Step 1.   Divide the numbers.

$$\frac{-6x^3y^2z}{-3xz} = 2$$

Step 2.   Divide the variables.
Divide the x's by subtracting exponents.

$$\frac{-6x^3y^2z}{-3xz} = 2x^2$$

Divide the y's.
There is no y in the denominator, so simply write y^2
in the answer.

$$\frac{-6x^3y^2z}{-3xz} = 2x^2y^2$$

Divide the z's.
The z's cancel each other out.

$$\frac{-6x^3y^2\cancel{z}}{-3x\cancel{z}} = 2x^2y^2$$

So, $\dfrac{-6x^3y^2z}{-3xz} = 2x^2y^2$

Example 2. $\dfrac{9ab^3c}{-ab} =$

    Step 1.   Divide the numbers.

$$\frac{9ab^3c}{-1ab} = -9$$

    Step 2.   Divide the variables by subtracting exponents.
The a's cancel out.

$$\frac{9\cancel{a}b^3c}{-1\cancel{a}b} = -9$$

Divide the b's.

$$\frac{9ab^3c}{-1ab} = -9b^2$$

Divide the c's.
There is no c in the denominator, so write c in the answer.

$$\frac{9ab^3c}{-1ab} = -9b^2c$$

So, $\dfrac{9ab^3c}{-ab} = -9b^2c$

Exercise 7

Divide these monomials.

1. $\dfrac{c^6}{c^4} =$

2. $\dfrac{a^4b^3c}{a^2bc} =$

3. $\dfrac{18d^2}{-6d^2} =$

4. $\dfrac{4p^2r^2}{-2p^2} =$

5. $\dfrac{-8rt}{-2r} =$

6. $\dfrac{5c^6d^2}{-d} =$

7. $\dfrac{16c^8}{-16c^8} =$

8. $\dfrac{m^2n^4}{mn^2s} =$

Answers for exercise 7

1. $\dfrac{c^6}{c^4} = c^2$

2. $\dfrac{a^4b^3c}{a^2bc} = a^2b^2$

3. $\dfrac{18d^2}{-6d^2} = -3$

4. $\dfrac{4p^2r^2}{-2p^2} = -2r^2$

5. $\dfrac{-8rt}{-2r} = 4t$

6. $\dfrac{5c^6d^2}{-d} = -5c^6d$

7. $\dfrac{16c^8}{-16c^8} = -1$

8. $\dfrac{m^2n^4}{mn^2s} = \dfrac{mn^2}{s}$

8. Adding polynomials together

Polynomials are expressions with more than one term.
Polynomials look like this:

$x^2 + 2xy - 5y^2$ This polynomial has three terms.

$4x^2 - 3xy + 6z^2$ This polynomial has three terms.

$4x^2 - 4y - 2y^2 + 7$ This polynomial has four terms.

Adding polynomials is very similar to adding monomials.
You can add only like terms.

Add: $(x^2 + 2xy - 5y^2) + (4x^2 - 3xy + 7y^2) =$

Step 1.   Write the problem so that like terms are in the same columns.

$$\begin{array}{r} x^2 + 2xy - 5y^2 \\ + 4x^2 - 3xy + 7y^2 \\ \hline \end{array}$$

Step 2.   Add each column.

$$\begin{array}{r} x^2 + 2xy - 5y^2 \\ + 4x^2 - 3xy + 7y^2 \\ \hline 5x^2 - xy + 2y^2 \end{array}$$

So, $(x^2 + 2xy - 5y^2) + (4x^2 - 3xy + 7y^2) = 5x^2 - xy + 2y^2$

Practice adding polynomials

Example 1.   Add: $(4a^2b^2 - 2a^2b + 3c) + (2a^2b^2 + 6a^2b - 8cd) =$

Step 1.   Set up the polynomials so that like terms are in the same columns.
If there aren't like terms, leave the space empty.

$$\begin{array}{r} 4a^2b^2 - 2a^2b + 3c \\ + 2a^2b^2 + 6a^2b \qquad - 8cd \\ \hline \end{array}$$

Step 2.   Add the columns.

$$\begin{array}{r} 4a^2b^2 - 2a^2b + 3c \\ + 2a^2b^2 + 6a^2b \qquad - 8cd \\ \hline 6a^2b^2 + 4a^2b + 3c - 8cd \end{array}$$

So, $(4a^2b^2 - 2a^2b + 3c) + (2a^2b^2 + 6a^2b - 8cd) =$
$6a^2b^2 + 4a^2b + 3c - 8cd$

Example 2. Add: $(3c^2 - 4c - 7) + (2c^2 + 2c + 2) + (-7c^2 + 5c - 8) =$

Step 1. Write columns of like terms.

$$
\begin{array}{r}
3c^2 - 4c - 7 \\
2c^2 + 2c + 2 \\
+ \ -7c^2 + 5c - 8 \\
\hline
\end{array}
$$

Step 2. Add.

$$
\begin{array}{r}
3c^2 - 4c - \ 7 \\
2c^2 + 2c + \ 2 \\
+ \ -7c^2 + 5c - \ 8 \\
\hline
-2c^2 + 3c - 13 \\
\end{array}
$$

So, $(3c^2 - 4c - 7) + (2c^2 + 2c + 2) + (-7c^2 + 5c - 8) =$
$-2c^2 + 3c - 13$

Exercise 8

Add these polynomials.

1. $(8y + 4) + (4y + 3) =$

2. $(2x^2 + 3xy - 4y^2) + (-3x^2 + 4xy + 2y^2) + (-2x^2 + 7xy + 3y^2) =$

3. $(3a + 4b) + (-2a - 3b) =$

4. $(5a + 6b - 8c) + (3a - 2b + d) =$

5. $(7c^2 + 4cd + 3) + (4c^2 - 4cd - 3) =$

6. $(9p + 4rs) + (5p - 5rs) + (7p + 4rs) =$

7. $(3c^2 + 4c - 8d) + (-2c^2 + 3c + 6d) =$

8. $(8r^2 + 3rs - 5st) + (r^2 - 3rs - 4s) =$

Answers for exercise 8

1. $(8y + 4) + (4y + 3) =$

$$\begin{array}{r} 8y + 4 \\ +\ 4y + 3 \\ \hline 12y + 7 \end{array}$$

2. $(2x^2 + 3xy - 4y^2) + (-3x^2 + 4xy + 2y^2) + (-2x^2 + 7xy + 3y^2) =$

$$\begin{array}{r} 2x^2 + 3xy - 4y^2 \\ -3x^2 + 4xy + 2y^2 \\ +\ -2x^2 + 7xy + 3y^2 \\ \hline -3x^2 + 14xy + y^2 \end{array}$$

3. $(3a + 4b) + (-2a - 3b) =$

$$\begin{array}{r} 3a + 4b \\ +\ -2a - 3b \\ \hline a + b \end{array}$$

4. $(5a + 6b - 8c) + (3a - 2b + d) =$

$$\begin{array}{r} 5a + 6b - 8c \\ +\ 3a - 2b \qquad + d \\ \hline 8a + 4b - 8c + d \end{array}$$

5. $(7c^2 + 4cd + 3) + (4c^2 - 4cd - 3) =$

$$\begin{array}{r} 7c^2 + 4cd + 3 \\ +\ 4c^2 - 4cd - 3 \\ \hline 11c^2 + 0 \quad + 0 = 11c^2 \end{array}$$

6. $(9p + 4rs) + (5p - 5rs) + (7p + 4rs) =$

$$\begin{array}{r} 9p + 4rs \\ 5p - 5rs \\ +\ 7p + 4rs \\ \hline 21p + 3rs \end{array}$$

7. $(3c^2 + 4c - 8d) + (-2c^2 + 3c + 6d) =$

$$\begin{array}{r} 3c^2 + 4c - 8d \\ +\ -2c^2 + 3c + 6d \\ \hline c^2 + 7c - 2d \end{array}$$

8. $(8r^2 + 3rs - 5st) + (r^2 - 3rs - 4s) =$

$$\begin{array}{r} 8r^2 + 3rs - 5st \\ +\ r^2 - 3rs \qquad - 4s \\ \hline 9r^2 + 0 \quad - 5st - 4s = 9r^2 - 5st - 4s \end{array}$$

9. Subtracting polynomials

Follow the rules for subtracting signed numbers when you subtract polynomials. Change the sign of the item you are subtracting, then add.

When you change signs of polynomials, change the signs of *all* the terms in the polynomial.

Subtract: $(4x^2 - 5xy - y^2) - (3x^2 + 5xy + y^2) =$

Step 1.   Put like terms in columns.

$$\begin{array}{r} 4x^2 - 5xy - y^2 \\ - \ (3x^2 + 5xy + y^2) \\ \hline \end{array}$$

Step 2.   Change the signs of all the terms in the bottom polynomial. Then add.

$$\begin{array}{r} 4x^2 - 5xy - y^2 \\ + \ -3x^2 - 5xy - y^2 \\ \hline x^2 - 10xy - 2y^2 \end{array}$$

So, $(4x^2 - 5xy - y^2) - (3x^2 + 5xy + y^2) = x^2 - 10xy - 2y^2$

Practice subtracting polynomials

Example 1. $(m^2 + 3m - 4mn) - (3m^2 + 8mn) =$

Step 1.   Line up like terms in columns.

$$\begin{array}{r} m^2 + 3m - 4mn \\ - \ (3m^2 \qquad + 8mn) \\ \hline \end{array}$$

Step 2.   Change the signs of all the terms in the bottom polynomial. Then add.

$$\begin{array}{r} m^2 + 3m - 4mn \\ + \ -3m^2 \qquad - 8mn \\ \hline -2m^2 + 3m - 12mn \end{array}$$

So, $(m^2 + 3m - 4mn) - (3m^2 + 8mn) =$
$-2m^2 + 3m - 12mn$

Example 2. $(7d^2 + 4c^2) - (4d^2 - 7c^2 + 3g) =$

Step 1.   Put like terms in columns.

$$\begin{array}{r} 7d^2 + 4c^2 \\ -4d^2 - 7c^2 + 3g \\ \hline \end{array}$$

Step 2.   Change the signs of all the terms in the second polynomial.
Then add.

$$\begin{array}{r} 7d^2 + 4c^2 \\ + -4d^2 + 7c^2 - 3g \\ \hline 3d^2 + 11c^2 - 3g \end{array}$$

So, $(7d^2 + 4c^2) - (4d^2 - 7c^2 + 3g) =$
$3d^2 + 11c^2 - 3g$

Exercise 9

Subtract these polynomials.

1. $(4d + 8e) - (3d - 5e) =$

2. $(6d^2 + 7e^2) - (3d^2 + 4e^2) =$

3. $(7x^2 + 3x) - (3x^2 - 4x - 4) =$

4. $(4b^2 - 3c + 4) - (3b^2 - 3c + 8) =$

5. $(2b^2 - 4c^2 + 6d^2) - (b^2 + c^2 - d^2) =$

6. $(5m^2 + 3mn + n^2) - (3m^2 + 4mn - n^2) =$

7. $(10pr + 8st) - (3pr - 3st - 4) =$

8. $(5x + 3y - 4z) - (2x + 7y + 4z) =$

Answers for exercise 9

1. $(4d + 8e) - (3d - 5e) =$

$$
\begin{array}{r}
4d + 8e \\
+ \;\; -3d + 5e \\
\hline
d + 13e
\end{array}
$$

2. $(6d^2 + 7e^2) - (3d^2 + 4e^2) =$

$$
\begin{array}{r}
6d^2 + 7e^2 \\
+ \;\; -3d^2 - 4e^2 \\
\hline
3d^2 + 3e^2
\end{array}
$$

3. $(7x^2 + 3x) - (3x^2 - 4x - 4) =$

$$
\begin{array}{r}
7x^2 + 3x \\
+ \;\; -3x^2 + 4x + 4 \\
\hline
4x^2 + 7x + 4
\end{array}
$$

4. $(4b^2 - 3c + 4) - (3b^2 - 3c + 8) =$

$$
\begin{array}{r}
4b^2 - 3c + 4 \\
+ \;\; -3b^2 + 3c - 8 \\
\hline
b^2 + 0 - 4 = b^2 - 4
\end{array}
$$

5. $(2b^2 - 4c^2 + 6d^2) - (b^2 + c^2 - d^2) =$

$$
\begin{array}{r}
2b^2 - 4c^2 + 6d^2 \\
+ \;\; -b^2 - c^2 + d^2 \\
\hline
b^2 - 5c^2 + 7d^2
\end{array}
$$

6. $(5m^2 + 3mn + n^2) - (3m^2 + 4mn - n^2) =$

$$
\begin{array}{r}
5m^2 + 3mn + n^2 \\
+ \;\; -3m^2 - 4mn + n^2 \\
\hline
2m^2 - mn + 2n^2
\end{array}
$$

7. $(10pr + 8st) - (3pr - 3st - 4) =$

$$
\begin{array}{r}
10pr + 8st \\
+ \;\; -3pr + 3st + 4 \\
\hline
7pr + 11st + 4
\end{array}
$$

8. $(5x + 3y - 4z) - (2x + 7y + 4z) =$

$$
\begin{array}{r}
5x + 3y - 4z \\
+ \;\; -2x - 7y - 4z \\
\hline
3x - 4y - 8z
\end{array}
$$

10. Multiplying polynomials by monomials

To multiply a polynomial by a monomial, multiply each term of the polynomial by the monomial.
Follow the rules for multiplying signed numbers.

Multiply: $-4(4b^2 - 5bc + 3c^2) =$

Step 1.   Set up the problem.
$$(4b^2 - 5bc + 3c^2)$$
$$\underline{\hspace{5cm} -4}$$

Step 2.   Multiply each term of the polynomial by -4.
Start at the left.
$$(4b^2 - 5bc + 3c^2)$$
$$\underline{\hspace{5cm} -4}$$
$$-16b^2$$

Step 3.   Multiply the second term by -4.
$$(4b^2 - 5bc + 3c^2)$$
$$\underline{\hspace{5cm} -4}$$
$$-16b^2 + 20bc$$

Step 4.   Multiply the third term by -4.
$$(4b^2 - 5bc + 3c^2)$$
$$\underline{\hspace{5cm} -4}$$
$$-16b^2 + 20bc - 12c^2$$

So, $-4(4b^2 - 5bc + 3c^2) = -16b^2 + 20bc - 12c^2$

You could also solve the same problem horizontally.

Step 1.   Multiply the first term of the polynomial by -4.
$$-4(4b^2 - 5bc + 3c^2) = -16b^2$$

Step 2.   Multiply the second term by -4.
$$-4(4b^2 - 5bc + 3c^2) = -16b^2 + 20bc$$

Step 3.   Multiply the third term by -4.
$$-4(4b^2 - 5bc + 3c^2) = -16b^2 + 20bc - 12c^2$$

Practice multiplying polynomials by monomials

Example 1.   Multiply: $ac(4ac + 7a - 3c) =$

Step 1.   Multiply the first term of the polynomial by ac.
To multiply, add exponents; if there is no exponent,
an exponent of 1 is understood.

$$ac(4ac + 7a - 3c) = 4a^2c^2$$

Step 2.   Multiply the second term of the polynomial by ac.

$$ac(4ac + 7a - 3c) = 4a^2c^2 + 7a^2c$$

Step 3.   Multiply the third term of the polynomial by ac.

$$ac(4ac + 7a - 3c) = 4a^2c^2 + 7a^2c - 3ac^2$$

So, $ac(4ac + 7a - 3c) = 4a^2c^2 + 7a^2c - 3ac^2$

Example 2.   Multiply: $4ab(3a + 2ab - 3b^2) =$

Step 1.   Multiply the first term of the polynomial by $4ab$.
$$(3a + 2ab - 3b^2)$$
$$\underline{\qquad\qquad 4ab}$$
$$12a^2b$$

Step 2.   Multiply the second term of the polynomial by $4ab$.
$$(3a + 2ab - 3b^2)$$
$$\underline{\qquad\qquad 4ab}$$
$$12a^2b + 8a^2b^2$$

Step 3.   Multiply the third term of the polynomial by $4ab$.
$$(3a + 2ab - 3b^2)$$
$$\underline{\qquad\qquad 4ab}$$
$$12a^2b + 8a^2b^2 - 12ab^3$$

So, $4ab(3a + 2ab - 3b^2) = 12a^2b + 8a^2b^2 - 12ab^3$

Example 3.   Multiply: $-2m(5m + 3) =$

$$-2m(5m + 3) = -10m^2 - 6m$$

Exercise 10

Multiply these expressions.

1. $4(x - 3) =$

2. $5(2b - 3d) =$

3. $b(b + 4) =$

4. $-3(2ab + 4b) =$

5. $-y^2(y^2 + y + 4) =$

6. $ab(4ab + 3a - 4b) =$

7. $3ad(4ad - 2a + 4d) =$

8. $2x^2y(2x^2y^2 - 4xy - 8) =$

Answers for exercise 10

1. $4(x - 3) = 4x - 12$

2. $5(2b - 3d) = 10b - 15d$

3. $b(b + 4) = b^2 + 4b$

4. $-3(2ab + 4b) = -6ab - 12b$

5. $-y^2(y^2 + y + 4) = -y^4 - y^3 - 4y^2$

6. $ab(4ab + 3a - 4b) = 4a^2b^2 + 3a^2b - 4ab^2$

7. $3ad(4ad - 2a + 4d) = 12a^2d^2 - 6a^2d + 12ad^2$

8. $2x^2y(2x^2y^2 - 4xy - 8) = 4x^4y^3 - 8x^3y^2 - \cdot 16x^2y$

11. Multiplying polynomials by polynomials

$(x + 3)(x + 2) =$

In this problem you are multiplying a polynomial by a polynomial.

Multiply each term of one polynomial by each term of the other polynomial.

Step 1.   Set up the problem vertically.

$$(x + 3)$$
$$(x + 2)$$

Step 2.   Multiply $(x + 3)$ by x.
Start at the left.

$$(x + 3)$$
$$(x + 2)$$
$$\overline{x^2 + 3x}$$

Step 3.   Multiply $(x + 3)$ by 2.
Keep like terms in columns.

$$(x + 3)$$
$$(x + 2)$$
$$\overline{x^2 + 3x}$$
$$\underline{ 2x + 6}$$

Step 4.   Add like terms.

$$(x + 3)$$
$$(x + 2)$$
$$\overline{x^2 + 3x}$$
$$\underline{ 2x + 6}$$
$$x^2 + 5x + 6$$

So, $(x + 3)(x + 2) = x^2 + 5x + 6$

You can also solve the problem horizontally.

$(x + 3)(x + 2) =$

Step 1.   Multiply $(x + 2)$ by the x in the first polynomial.

$$(x + 3)(x + 2) = x^2 + 2x$$

Step 2.   Multiply $(x + 2)$ by 3.

$$(x + 3)(x + 2) = x^2 + 2x + 3x + 6$$

Step 3.   Combine any like terms.

$$x^2 + 2x + 3x + 6 = x^2 + 5x + 6$$

So, $(x + 3)(x + 2) = x^2 + 5x + 6$

Practice multiplying polynomials by polynomials

Example 1. $(7c + d)(7c - d) =$

Step 1.   Multiply $(7c + d)$ by $7c$.

$$(7c + d)$$
$$(7c - d)$$
$$\overline{49c^2 + 7cd}$$

Step 2.   Multiply $(7c + d)$ by $-d$.

$$(7c + d)$$
$$(7c - d)$$
$$\overline{49c^2 + 7cd}$$
$$\underline{\quad - 7cd - d^2}$$

Step 3.   Add any like terms.

$$(7c + d)$$
$$(7c - d)$$
$$\overline{49c^2 + 7cd}$$
$$\underline{\quad\quad - 7cd - d^2}$$
$$49c^2 + 0 \quad - d^2 = 49c^2 - d^2$$

So, $(7c + d)(7c - d) = 49c^2 - d^2$

Example 2. $(4x^2 + 3xy - 2y^2)(6x - 2y) =$

Step 1.   Multiply $(4x^2 + 3xy - 2y^2)$ by $6x$.

$$(4x^2 + 3xy - 2y^2)$$
$$(6x - 2y)$$
$$\overline{24x^3 + 18x^2y - 12xy^2}$$

Step 2.   Multiply $(4x^2 + 3xy - 2y^2)$ by $-2y$.

$$(4x^2 + 3xy - 2y^2)$$
$$(6x - 2y)$$
$$\overline{24x^3 + 18x^2y - 12xy^2}$$
$$\underline{\quad - 8x^2y - 6xy^2 + 4y^3}$$

Step 3.   Add like terms.

$$(4x^2 + 3xy - 2y^2)$$
$$(6x - 2y)$$
$$\overline{24x^3 + 18x^2y - 12xy^2}$$
$$\underline{+ \quad - 8x^2y - 6xy^2 + 4y^3}$$
$$24x^3 + 10x^2y - 18xy^2 + 4y^3$$

So, $(4x^2 + 3xy - 2y^2)(6x - 2y) =$
$$24x^3 + 10x^2y - 18xy^2 + 4y^3$$

Exercise 11

Multiply these polynomials.

1. $(c + 2)(c - 5) =$

2. $(x - 4)(x - 5) =$

3. $(3x - y)(4x + y) =$

4. $(5m + 4n)(3m - 6n) =$

5. $(4b^2 - b)(2b^2 + 3b) =$

6. $(4p^2 + 4)(8p^2 + 8) =$

7. $(5m^2 - 4mn - 3n^2)(8m + 2n) =$

8. $(4p^2 - 7pt + 5t^2)(3p - 6t) =$

Answers for exercise 11

1. $(c + 2)(c - 5) =$

$(c + 2)$
$(c - 5)$

$c^2 + 2c$
$\quad\quad - 5c - 10$

$c^2 - 3c - 10$

2. $(x - 4)(x - 5) =$

$(x - 4)$
$(x - 5)$

$x^2 - 4x$
$\quad\quad - 5x + 20$

$x^2 - 9x + 20$

3. $(3x - y)(4x + y) =$

$(3x - y)$
$(4x + y)$

$12x^2 - 4xy$
$\quad\quad + 3xy - y^2$

$12x^2 - xy - y^2$

4. $(5m + 4n)(3m - 6n) =$

$(5m + 4n)$
$(3m - 6n)$

$15m^2 + 12mn$
$\quad\quad - 30mn - 24n^2$

$15m^2 - 18mn - 24n^2$

5. $(4b^2 - b)(2b^2 + 3b) =$

$(4b^2 - b)$
$(2b^2 + 3b)$

$8b^4 - 2b^3$
$\quad\quad + 12b^3 - 3b^2$

$8b^4 + 10b^3 - 3b^2$

6. $(4p^2 + 4)(8p^2 + 8) =$

$(4p^2 + 4)$
$(8p^2 + 8)$

$32p^4 + 32p^2$
$\quad\quad + 32p^2 + 32$

$32p^4 + 64p^2 + 32$

7. $(5m^2 - 4mn - 3n^2)(8m + 2n) =$

$(5m^2 - 4mn - 3n^2)$
$\quad\quad\quad (8m + 2n)$

$40m^3 - 32m^2n - 24mn^2$
$\quad\quad\quad 10m^2n - 8mn^2 - 6n^3$

$40m^3 - 22m^2n - 32mn^2 - 6n^3$

8. $(4p^2 - 7pt + 5t^2)(3p - 6t) =$

$(4p^2 - 7pt + 5t^2)$
$\quad\quad\quad (3p - 6t)$

$12p^3 - 21p^2t + 15pt^2$
$\quad\quad\quad - 24p^2t + 42pt^2 - 30t^3$

$12p^3 - 45p^2t + 57pt^2 - 30t^3$

12. Dividing polynomials by monomials

To divide a polynomial by a monomial, divide each term of the polynomial by the monomial.

To divide, you subtract exponents.

$$\frac{15b^3 - 21b^2 - 9b}{3b} =$$

Step 1.   Divide the first term of the polynomial by $3b$.

$$\frac{15b^3 - 21b^2 - 9b}{3b} = 5b^2$$

Step 2.   Divide the second term by $3b$.

$$\frac{15b^3 - 21b^2 - 9b}{3b} = 5b^2 - 7b$$

Step 3.   Divide the third term by $3b$.

$$\frac{15b^3 - 21b^2 - 9b}{3b} = 5b^2 - 7b - 3$$

So, $\dfrac{15b^3 - 21b^2 - 9b}{3b} = 5b^2 - 7b - 3$

Practice dividing polynomials by monomials

Example 1. $\dfrac{8x^4y^3 + 4x^3y^2 - x^2y}{x^2y} =$

Step 1.   Divide the first term by x^2y.

$$\frac{8x^4y^3 + 4x^3y^2 - x^2y}{x^2y} = 8x^2y^2$$

Step 2.   Divide the second term by x^2y.

$$\frac{8x^4y^3 + 4x^3y^2 - x^2y}{x^2y} = 8x^2y^2 + 4xy$$

Step 3.   Divide the last term by x^2y.

$$\frac{8x^4y^3 + 4x^3y^2 - x^2y}{x^2y} = 8x^2y^2 + 4xy - 1$$

So, $\dfrac{8x^4y^3 + 4x^3y^2 - x^2y}{x^2y} = 8x^2y^2 + 4xy - 1$

Example 2. $\dfrac{m^4 - m^3}{m} =$

   Step 1.   Divide the first term by m.

   $$\dfrac{m^4 - m^3}{m} = m^3$$

   Step 2.   Divide the second term by m.

   $$\dfrac{m^4 - m^3}{m} = m^3 - m^2$$

   So, $\dfrac{m^4 - m^3}{m} = m^3 - m^2$

Exercise 12

Divide these terms.

1. $\dfrac{10m^3 - 15mn}{5m} =$

2. $\dfrac{4p + 8p}{4p} =$

3. $\dfrac{2x - 8x^2}{-x} =$

4. $\dfrac{8d^2 - d}{-d} =$

5. $\dfrac{3a^2b - 9ab + 12ab^2}{3ab} =$

6. $\dfrac{x^2y - 5x^3y^2 + 3x^4y^3}{x^2y} =$

7. $\dfrac{10m^3 - m^2}{-m} =$

8. $\dfrac{12x^3 - 24x^2 + 8x}{-4x} =$

Answers for exercise 12

1. $\dfrac{10m^3 - 15mn}{5m} = 2m^2 - 3n$

2. $\dfrac{4p + 8p}{4p} = 1 + 2 = 3$

3. $\dfrac{2x - 8x^2}{-x} = -2 + 8x$

4. $\dfrac{8d^2 - d}{-d} = -8d + 1$

5. $\dfrac{3a^2b - 9ab + 12ab^2}{3ab} = a - 3 + 4b$

6. $\dfrac{x^2y - 5x^3y^2 + 3x^4y^3}{x^2y} = 1 - 5xy + 3x^2y^2$

7. $\dfrac{10m^3 - m^2}{-m} = -10m^2 + m$

8. $\dfrac{12x^3 - 24x^2 + 8x}{-4x} = -3x^2 + 6x - 2$

13. Finding factors of terms with variables

Factors are numbers or variables which, when multiplied together, produce a given term.

What are the factors of $16a^2b$?
That is, what numbers or variables, when multiplied together, equal $16a^2b$?

Step 1.   Find the factors of 16.
$$16 = (1)(16)$$
$$(2)(8)$$
$$(4)(4)$$

Step 2.   Find the factors of a^2b.
$$a^2b = (a^2)(b)$$
$$(a)(a)(b)$$

So, the factors of $16a^2b$ are 1, 2, 4, 8, 16, a, a^2, and b.

To find the factors of a polynomial, first find the highest common factor of all the terms in the polynomial.
The highest common factor is the highest term that will divide evenly into all the terms of the polynomial.

Factor: $(16a^2b + 24a^2c + 28a^2d)$.

Step 1.   Find the highest common factor for the numbers in front of the terms.

$$16 = (1)(16) \qquad 24 = (1)(24) \qquad 28 = (1)(28)$$
$$(2)(8) \qquad\qquad (2)(12) \qquad\qquad (2)(14)$$
$$(4)(4) \qquad\qquad (3)(8) \qquad\qquad (4)(7)$$
$$(4)(6)$$

The three numbers have 1, 2, and 4 in common.
But, the *highest* common factor is 4.

Step 2.   Find the highest common factor for the variables.

$$a^2b = (a)(a)(b) \qquad a^2c = (a)(a)(c) \qquad a^2d = (a)(a)(d)$$
$$(a^2)(b) \qquad\qquad (a^2)(c) \qquad\qquad (a^2)(d)$$

a and a^2 are common to all three.
But a^2 is the *highest* common factor for the variables.

Step 3.   Put the letter factor next to the number factor: $4a^2$.
$4a^2$ is the highest common factor for all the terms of the polynomial.

Step 4.   Divide the polynomial by the highest common factor.

$$\frac{16a^2b + 24a^2c + 28a^2d}{4a^2} = 4b + 6c + 7d$$

So, the factors of $(16a^2b + 24a^2c + 28a^2d)$ are:
$4a^2$ and $(4b + 6c + 7d)$.
Write the factors like this: $4a^2(4b + 6c + 7d)$.

Practice factoring terms with letters

Example 1. Factor: $(rst + rsw + rsz)$.

Step 1. Find the highest common factor.
Since there are no numbers in the terms, find the variables that all the terms of the polynomial have in common.
$$rst = (r)(s)(t) \qquad rsw = (r)(s)(w) \qquad rsz = (r)(s)(z)$$
All the terms have r and s in common.
So, the highest common factor is rs.

Step 2. Divide the polynomial by the highest common factor.
$$\frac{rst + rsw + rsz}{rs} = t + w + z$$
So, the factors of $(rst + rsw + rsz)$ are:
$$rs(t + w + z).$$

Example 2. Factor: $(10a^2bc - 15a^2b^2c^2 + 5a^2b^3c^3)$.

Step 1. Factor the numbers and find the highest common factor.
$$10 = (1)(10) \qquad 15 = (1)(15) \qquad 5 = (1)(5)$$
$$(2)(5) \qquad\qquad (3)(5)$$
The common factors are 1 and 5; the highest common factor is 5.

Step 2. Find the highest common factor for the variables.
Look at the three terms: a^2bc, $a^2b^2c^2$, $a^2b^3c^3$.
What variables are common to all three?
All three have a^2 in them.
They all have b and c in them.
So, the highest common factor for the variables is a^2bc.

Step 3. Write the variables next to the number factor.
$5a^2bc$ is the highest common factor of all the terms in the polynomial.

Step 4. Divide the polynomial by the highest common factor.
$$\frac{10a^2bc - 15a^2b^2c^2 + 5a^2b^3c^3}{5a^2bc} = 2 - 3bc + b^2c^2$$
So, the factors of $(10a^2bc - 15a^2b^2c^2 + 5a^2b^3c^3)$ are:
$$5a^2bc(2 - 3bc + b^2c^2).$$

Exercise 13

Factor these polynomials.

1. $(4b + 4d)$

2. $(3r - 9)$

3. $(b^3 - b^2)$

4. $(4pr + 8pt)$

5. $(5x^3 + 10x^2 - 15x)$

6. $(m^2n - mn^2 + mn^3)$

7. $(4x^2y - 16x^3y^2 + 24x^4y^3)$

8. $(a^2bc - ab^2c + abc^2)$

Answers for exercise 13

1. $(4b + 4d) = 4(b + d)$

2. $(3r - 9) = 3(r - 3)$

3. $(b^3 - b^2) = b^2(b - 1)$

4. $(4pr + 8pt) = 4p(r + 2t)$

5. $(5x^3 + 10x^2 - 15x) = 5x(x^2 + 2x - 3)$

6. $(m^2n - mn^2 + mn^3) = mn(m - n + n^2)$

7. $(4x^2y - 16x^3y^2 + 24x^4y^3) = 4x^2y(1 - 4xy + 6x^2y^2)$

8. $(a^2bc - ab^2c + abc^2) = abc(a - b + c)$

14. Multiplying the sum and difference of two numbers

This is the sum of two numbers: $a + 3$.

This is the difference of the same two numbers: $a - 3$.

Multiply them as you would multiply any two polynomials.

$(a + 3)(a - 3) =$

$$
\begin{array}{l}
(a + 3) \\
\underline{(a - 3)} \\
a^2 + 3a \\
\underline{\quad - 3a - 9} \\
a^2 + 0 \; - 9 = a^2 - 9
\end{array}
$$

So, $(a + 3)(a - 3) = a^2 - 9$

You can take a shortcut when you multiply the sum and difference of two numbers. Square the first number and then subtract the square of the second number.

Multiply: $(x + 5)(x - 5) =$

Step 1.　Square the first number.

x^2

Step 2.　Square the second number and then subtract it from the square of the first number.

$x^2 - 25$

So, $(x + 5)(x - 5) = x^2 - 25$

You would get the same answer if you multiplied it all out.

$(x + 5)(x - 5) =$

$$
\begin{array}{l}
(x + 5) \\
\underline{(x - 5)} \\
x^2 + 5x \\
\underline{\quad - 5x - 25} \\
x^2 + 0 \; - 25 = x^2 - 25
\end{array}
$$

When you multiply the sum and difference of the same two numbers, you will always get a 0 in the middle.
So, you can use the shortcut.

Practice multiplying the sum and difference of two numbers

Example 1. $(a + 2)(a - 2) =$

Step 1. Square the first number.

a^2

Step 2. Square the second number and subtract it from the square of the first.

$a^2 - 4$

So, $(a + 2)(a - 2) = a^2 - 4$

Example 2. $(x^2 + y)(x^2 - y) =$

Step 1. Square the first number

x^4

Step 2. Square the second number and subtract it from the square of the first number.

$x^4 - y^2$

So, $(x^2 + y)(x^2 - y) = x^4 - y^2$

Exercise 14

Multiply the sum and difference of these numbers.

1. $(m + n^2)(m - n^2) =$

2. $(z + 7)(z - 7) =$

3. $(y + 7n)(y - 7n) =$

4. $(3z + 3x)(3z - 3x) =$

5. $(ab + c)(ab - c) =$

Answers for exercise 14

1. $(m + n^2)(m - n^2) = m^2 - n^4$

2. $(z + 7)(z - 7) = z^2 - 49$

3. $(y + 7n)(y - 7n) = y^2 - 49n^2$

4. $(3z + 3x)(3z - 3x) = 9z^2 - 9x^2$

5. $(ab + c)(ab - c) = a^2b^2 - c^2$

15. Factoring the difference of two squares

When you multiply $(x + 5)(x - 5)$, the product is $x^2 - 25$.
That product is the *difference of two squares*.
The difference of two squares is one square subtracted from another square.
$x^2 - 9$ is the difference of two squares.
$x^2y^2 - x^2$ is the differences of two squares.

Both terms in the expression must be perfect squares.
You must be able to find a whole number square root for any number and a square root for the variables.

Factoring the difference of two squares is the opposite of multiplying the sum and difference of two numbers.

Factor: $(x^2 - 49)$.

Step 1.   Find the square root of x^2.
$$\sqrt{x^2} = x$$
Find the square root of 49.
$$\sqrt{49} = 7$$

Step 2.   Write the sum of those two square roots.
$(x + 7)$

Step 3.   Write the difference of those two square roots.
$(x - 7)$

Step 4.   Write the sum and difference next to each other.
$(x + 7)(x - 7)$
So, the factors of $(x^2 - 49)$ are: $(x + 7)(x - 7)$.

To factor the difference of two squares, find the square root of each term.
Then write the sum and difference of those two terms.

Practice factoring the difference of two squares

Example 1.   Factor: $(a^2 - b^2)$.

Step 1. a^2 and b^2 are both perfect squares.

Find the square root of a^2: $\sqrt{a^2} = a$.

Find the square root of b^2: $\sqrt{b^2} = b$.

Step 2.   Write the sum of the two square roots.
$(a + b)$

Step 3.   Write the difference of those two square roots.
$(a - b)$

Step 4.   Write the sum and difference of the square roots next to each other.
$(a + b)(a - b)$
So, $(a^2 - b^2) = (a + b)(a - b)$

Example 2.   Factor: $(100x^2 - 81y^2)$.

Step 1.   Find the square root of $100x^2$: $\sqrt{100x^2} = 10x$

Find the square root of $81y^2$: $\sqrt{81y^2} = 9y$

Step 2.   Write the sum of the two square roots.
$(10x + 9y)$

Step 3.   Write the difference of the two square roots.
$(10x - 9y)$

Step 4.   Write the sum and difference next to each other.
$(10x + 9y)(10x - 9y)$
So, $100x^2 - 81y^2 = (10x + 9y)(10x - 9y)$

Exercise 15

Factor these expressions.

1. $(b^2 - 49)$

2. $(25 - c^2)$

3. $(9b^2 - 25c^2)$

4. $(100p^2 - 16r^2)$

5. $(4x^2 - 36y^2)$

6. $(64s^2 - t^2)$

7. $(x^2 - y^2)$

8. $(36b^4 - c^2)$

Answers for exercise 15

1. $(b^2 - 49) = (b + 7)(b - 7)$

2. $(25 - c^2) = (5 + c)(5 - c)$

3. $(9b^2 - 25c^2) = (3b + 5c)(3b - 5c)$

4. $(100p^2 - 16r^2) = (10p + 4r)(10p - 4r)$

5. $(4x^2 - 36y^2) = (2x + 6y)(2x - 6y)$

6. $(64s^2 - t^2) = (8s + t)(8s - t)$

7. $(x^2 - y^2) = (x + y)(x - y)$

8. $(36b^4 - c^2) = (6b^2 + c)(6b^2 - c)$

Post-test

1. List the factors of -48.

_____

2. (Circle the right answer)
   -3^4 means
   a. $(-3)(-4)$
   b. $-3 + 4$
   c. $(-3)(-3)(-3)(-3)$

3. Find the value of 3^4: _____

4. $\sqrt{\frac{4}{9}}$ = _____

5. List the terms in this expression:
   $12mn - 5mn + 8ab^2 - 2y$

   _____

6. List any like terms in this expression:
   $3m^2 + 2m^2 - mn$

   _____

7. Combine: $9w + 3w$ = _____

8. Combine: $(8m^2) - (-8m^2)$ = _____

9. $(-c^2)(bc)$ = _____

10. $\dfrac{18a^2b^2}{3ab}$ = _____

11. $(9d - 3e - 5f) + (3d + 2e - 2f)$ =

    _____

12. $(d^2 + 4de) - (-3de + e^2)$ =

    _____

13. $3x(4x^2 + 3x - 1)$ =

    _____

14. $(x + 4)(x + 2)$ =

    _____

15. $\dfrac{d^3 - d^2}{d}$ = _____

16. Factor: $(20xy + 40x^2y^2)$

    _____

17. $(2x + 3y)(2x - 3y)$ =

    _____

18. Factor: $(4c^2 - 36)$

    _____

Answers for post-test

1. $\pm 1, \ \pm 2, \ \pm 3, \ \pm 4, \ \pm 6, \ \pm 8, \ \pm 12, \ \pm 16, \ \pm 24, \ \pm 48$

2. c

3. 81

4. $\dfrac{2}{3}$

5. $12mn, \ 5mn, \ 8ab^2, \ 2y$

6. $3m^2, \ 2m^2$

7. $12w$

8. $16m^2$

9. $-bc^3$

10. $6ab$

11. $12d - e - 7f$

12. $d^2 + 7de - e^2$

13. $12x^3 + 9x^2 - 3x$

14. $x^2 + 6x + 8$

15. $d^2 - d$

16. $20xy(1 + 2xy)$

17. $4x^2 - 9y^2$

18. $(2c + 6)(2c - 6)$

If you missed this question:	Go back to these pages:
1	6-8
2 or 3	9-12
4	13-15
5 or 6	16-18
7 or 8	19-22
9	23-27
10	28-32
11	33-35
12	36-38
13	39-42
14	43-46
15	47-49
16	50-53
17	54-56
18	57-60